❧Maiku❧

Copyright © 2014 by Sonya L. Williams

Maiku
by Sonya L. Williams

Printed in the United States of America

ISBN-978-0-9896940-3-2

All rights reserved solely by the author. The author guarantees all contents are original and do not infringe upon the legal rights of any other person or work. No part of this book may be reproduced in any form without permission of the author. The views expressed in this book are not necessarily those of the publisher.

Introduction

    I would first like to thank you for allowing me to share my love of poetry with you in my fifth published book. If you have read and enjoyed my previous collection of poetry in *Shawty Du-Write Haiku*, you will certainly love *Maiku*.

    Before, I tell you about *Maiku*, I want to thank God for giving me the ability to write and the opportunities to share this gift with others. I would also like to thank Micah Holmes, a very good friend of mine who actually inspired me to write this book, hence, the name; *Maiku*.

    For those who don't know, haiku poetry is a Japanese form of writing that consists of three lines with a pattern of five syllables, seven syllables, then five syllables. Though haiku poetry is often written about nature, I've taken the basic format along with my personal style of writing and made it my own.

    Upon reading *Shawty Du-Write Haiku*, Micah gave me the idea of creating flowing haiku, which includes the basic foundation of three lines and the five-seven-five syllable format, but it also builds into a lengthier piece that tells a story and paints a picture for the reader to perceive.

Thank you to all of my family, friends, supporters and fellow spoken word artists who have motivated me and encouraged me to continually take my writing to the next level. I'm so very appreciative of the friendships and partnerships that have been formed as I've continued to grow in this industry. Your love and support will never go without recognition. Thank you again. Enjoy and God bless.

Never Date Poets

My ex was crazy.
I drove my current insane
and let him tell it:

Ice flows through my veins.
I don't blame him for leavin,
I'da left me too!

I'd often profess
"I love you all the way to
the moon." Tide washed words.

Waves of emotion
would rise and fall with every
wind that blew my way.

Actions contradict
every word I say as if
I were born one way

yet raised another.
Now with reflections of my
father and mother

I'm fighting this war
to rewrite my history.
The mystery is:

How can I break free
if I forfeited the key:
communication?

Silence plus anger
is worse than violent acts.
It kills me softly.

While you live a lie,
I watch and swallow my pride,
knowing words can kill

and I can't afford
the bill my mouth would run up,
so I hold my peace.

But one things for sure
if I catch her in these streets,
I keep me a piece

with her name on it.
Tell Sestina and Sonnet
I'm 'bout to call Mic

to light this chick up.
Put her soul on blast so she
can rest in pieces

of your memory
as a reminder to you.
One word of advice:

Never date poets.
Xs and Os may become
exes in hate prose.

Keep It Movin

Every time I leave
you somehow convince me that
what I left behind

is actually
worth coming back to, as if
I can't find better.

You pull all the stops
trying to put me in a
sentimental mood.

Baby that train left
a long time ago, and if
you think I'm trippin'

watch me pack my bags
and keep it movin' like we
never even met.

Let Me Be Your Muse

If love is the script
and you are the producer,
let me be your muse.

Use me to loose the
tension you've been withholding.
Just let my lips mold

the tone of each scene.
Serenity at its best.
Lost in the essence

of creative prose.
I suppose with or without
closing this chapter.

I promise to keep
this sheet warm for only you.
You are the writer

and I am your script.
I trust I'm safe in your grip.
I'll let you just glide.

As long as your pen
respects the value inside
the pages it's filled.

Remember one thing;
until your name is on it
you can't prove it's yours.

So I wanna be
official. I wanna be
the reason you write

beautiful love songs,
poetry, novels and scripts
of our life story.

Love Is Blind

Dude ain't even fine,
but somehow his art inscribed
braille upon my heart.

His tongue is the key
to unlocking fantasies
I've never dreamed of.

His lips are warm clay.
My mind is a potter's wheel
spun out of control.

Disastrously
beautiful masterpieces
are born of this mess.

Mass of emotions
cooked in the kiln of my heart.
Some call it passion,

I call it live art
because it breathes life into
these dry bones of mine.

Dude ain't even fine!
But the way he got me gone,
I guess love is blind.

Teddy Bears

Christmas time is near
and you ask me what I want.
So then I ask you,

"Can you afford it?"
You give me this look as if
I just crushed your pride.

No, it's not like that.
I mean are you willing to
invest in this thing?

I want more than rings.
I need more than cars and though
I'd love to have kids,

that's not what I want
right now. My life is missing
something you don't have.

The cost is quite high
and it's not available
in department stores,

or even online.
It can't be bought with money
but it will cost time.

I want you close by
but I need you to fall back
because I'm tempted

to take a sneak peek
and see what you've got for me.
What you're offering

is only a piece
of what I know I deserve.
I'm willing to wait

'cause I want more than
a taste and I'd rather not
spoil my appetite.

I want all of you.
I need more than attention.
I need commitment.

I want to cuddle.
I want to hear the sound of
your heartbeat with mine.

I want to drift off
into last night's dream again.
You know that one when

we...wait, never mind.
This Christmas just get me a
little teddy bear.

You think I'm confused.
Well the truth is, I've been bruised
one too many times

and I refuse to
ever take that route again.
As much as I want

you here in my bed
I want even more for you
to be in my life,

for better or worse
in sickness and health, til death.
I want commitment.

I'm committed to
giving you something worthy
of all the waiting.

Trust, it will be sweet,
savory, succulent and
good to the last drop.

So let's try this one
more time. You ask what I want.
And I will tell you...

One mocha teddy.
To have and to hold on those
lonely winter nights,

as a reminder
that you're always there for me
despite the distance,

you're thinking of me,
and preparing for the day
when you'll take his place.

Two-Step

I just don't know what
to say so I speak in tongues;
praying lips connect

to the groaning of
my heart's deepest desires.
Intimate fires

burn within my soul
causing me to lose control
and let rivers flow.

Deep cries out to deep
as I await your presence.
Come to me, my love.

Wrap me in your arms
so I can hear your heartbeat
and dance to the sound.

Spin me around and
dip it low one time before
you then pull me close,

and now we'll slow wind.
I am yours and you are mine.
Together, we write

the perfect love song.
Like treble-makin' angels
fallen from Heaven,

we land on cloud nine.
That place where all time stands still
and I remember

the moment I took
your hand, thinking you could lead
me to paradise.

Instead, I rolled dice
and took a chance with my heart.
I gave you my love

while you gave me lust
wrapped in a pretty lil bow.
We're two steps away

yet ever so far
from the perfect love story,
but this is the end.

I say to myself
"Never will I fall into
temptation again."

Truth be told, I might
but one things for sure, I won't
make this mistake twice.

Minstrel Cycles

It's often said that
I can be quite difficult.
I'd have to agree

with you but trust me,
you don't even know the half.
You try waking up

to millions of thoughts
on replay, goals on delay,
simply because I

can't even think straight
when my mind goes left and my
heart wants to go right.

An ongoing fight
between my flesh and spirit
but no one hears it

and nobody knows
the trouble I've seen. They don't
even see me cry.

I guess in their eyes
I'm either strong, or a fool
to keep holding on

to anything that
they themselves would give up on.
Its "reality"

"facts" and "statistics".
It is what it is and I
should just get with it.

I'm not trying to
fit in; I live to stand out
and I won't back down

until I see the
promises of God revealed.
Call it what you want.

Depression? Maybe.
Obsession or ADD?
You don't even know.

Guess I'm just crazy.
Crazy enough to believe
every word God speaks.

Yes, He speaks to me
No, I'm not just hearing things
He speaks to you too;

you just don't listen.
You'd rather live by feelings
and the opinions

of people who don't
even have their own lives right.
Who's to say what's right?

'Cause in these last days
everyone's so quick to say
"You only live once

so get high today.
Who cares about tomorrow?
Live fast and die young."

No, I think I'll pass.
See, this fight that I've been in
is already fixed

and no matter what,
the victory is still mine.
I may get knocked down.

I might even lose
my mind but my heart is still
beating with His blood.

I'm willing to die
'cause the reward is new life
and what I may lose

is absolutely
nothing in comparison
to what I will gain.

I'm willing to wait
but I must participate.
I must walk by faith

and not be deterred
by what I see around me.
It's all a smoke screen

A plot to get me
thinking I've already lost
so I might forfeit.

I won't be deceived
by what I think, feel or see
'cause my faith stays locked

like pit bulls in heat.
Yeah I may have my moments.
At times I get weak

but then I find peace
when God manifests through me.
In Him I find strength

to wake up each day
knowing I have the chance to
rewrite history.

It's Not You, It's Me

It's not you, it's me.
I know that it sounds cliché
but, really, it's me.

Please don't take this as
some reverse psychology
way of saying that

"I'm just not that in
to you and rather than hurt
you, I'll lie to you,

butter you up and
insult your intelligence".
No, really, it's me.

Truth is, I like you.
But am I in love with you?
That don't even count

'cause being in love
is like having a sweet tooth.
It's a temporal

emotion that comes
and goes depending on the
matters of the heart.

Being in love is
a beautiful thing but I
can't get my hopes up

for something that won't
even last the test of time.
I'm willing to wait.

Question is, "Are you?"
If you're ready for the world
and I'm five heartbeats

away from climax
with or without your presence,
it's time to fall back.

You say you like risk
but trust me it ain't worth it.
I've been down that road

and it's a dead end.
Actually it's more like
a round-a-bout path

we continue to
follow until we're tired
of the same ol game.

Tired of getting
played and betrayed by those who
claim to love us most.

No, I'm not jaded
and I really do trust you.
It's me I don't trust.

I know I'm not quite
ready to give you my heart.
So it's in God's hands

and when you're ready
to take my hand in marriage
you'll find me right there,

patiently waiting
for the Lover of My Soul
to give me away.

It's not you, it's me.
I value my purity
and for this, I'll wait.

The Words: I love you

Sayin' I love you
is like nails in a coffin.
'cause it kills my flesh,

yet brings forth the best
of me. It's transparency
at its weakest point.

It strips me of my
power and gives you the key
to my deepest thoughts.

It paralyzes
my senses and I forget
the consequences

of speaking such truth.
Now I'm obligated to
practice what I preach.

Three words once spoken
are like seeds planted in the
hearts of those who hear.

I don't think I can
carry the weight of these words.
It's like word-vomit.

I can't control it
when my heart just erupts and
bypasses my mind

and somehow ends up
right in the palm of your hands.
Once again, I've put

my foot in my mouth.
I could kick myself for this!
But what would it help

to beat myself up
for simply speaking the truth.
Being, I love you.

Contrary to lust
whether its male or female
my love is the same

'cause I'm not looking
for anything to be gained
by our connection.

No need for sex and
back and forth textin' kisses
to show you my love.

It seems that these days
the definition has been
twisted into lies.

We "love" with our eyes,
yet fail to see what's inside.
So caught up in the

outer appearance
that when the truth comes to light,
we'd rather just hide.

Listen, that's not love.
That's lust wrapped up in a cute
bow of deception

aimed only to please
itself. With or without your
approval, it takes.

These words hold no weight
unless actions show and prove
themselves to be true.

So when I tell you
I love you, hold me to it.
Make sure I prove it.

I give you every
right to mark my words but if
ever I should fail,

I hope that your love
prevails in forgiving me
just as I would you.

I'm learning to love
above the standards of what
this world sets so low.

Solo Dolo is
what they claim to be but if
truth be told no one

really wants to be
alone. If that were the case,
why do we replace

every old flame with
attempts to keep ourselves warm?
If we only knew…

It is only the
love of God that can give us
ability to

love anyone else.

Without His love our words are nothing but vain breaths.

I Still Do

Is it vain to say
that I love my reflection
when light hits your eyes?

It gives me a glimpse
of what tomorrow can bring.
Something to strive for.

Something to die for,
and since you're taller than me,
something to rise for.

I think that your eyes
unlock the keys to your soul,
which was once so cold

but right when you glanced
my way I pray that I left
imprints on your heart

of visions that can't
be erased. Kisses that leave
my taste lingering

on your lips. Baby,
Carmex ain't got nothin on
these lips when I spit

what's been on my mind.
Sit back while I take you on
a ride and no doubt

I'm 'bout to show you
just how skydiving should be
if you're willing to

take the risk with me.
It's reckless abandonment
of what was once real

and what we both feel.
But the moment we let go
and step out on faith

free fallin' in grace
and flowing with the current
despite turbulence,

we soar like eagles.
Together, we can still rise.
Just don't close your eyes.

I want to see me
when I look into your eyes.
And when you see me

I want to reflect
God's love. Unconditional.
Unconventional.

Better than your last.
The type to make you forget
the scars of your past.

I wanna see us
when I go to sleep at night.
Dreaming of this night,

remembering the
moment that I took the mic
and said "I still do".

Visions of Love

When I was a child,
I had a vision of love
that painted pictures

I'll never forget.
Memories of deleted
scenes are forever

entangled in my
heart's strings. So every time he
strikes that chord, I shake.

Cold chills up my spine
and my heart drops to the floor.
This just can't be love.

There's no fear in love.
So why am I always stressed
and worried 'bout him?

Why am I concerned
what he might do while I'm gone?
Why am I trippin'?

Love holds no grudges.
Why am I holding onto
what was done back then?

I've forgiven them
but the memories remain
and these roots run deep.

They're deeper than the
superficial cracks that you
see on the surface.

This house was never
a home; it was more like a
preowned fantasy.

Previous tenants
blindly invested in love
not knowing its worth.

If they had known the
value, they never would've
walked away so soon.

Their focus was more
on the outer appearance
than the foundation

that would hold it up
when the storms of life hit hard.
And when those storms hit

their home was destroyed.
If they could only see the
blessing in this mess.

Falling to your knees
doesn't make you weak, instead
it puts you in the

perfect position
to see the roses blooming
through the cracked concrete.

More than just beauty
they represent the power
of agape love.

Despite the present
circumstances, they still bloom.
Deep within hard hearts

lives a seed that has
struggled to make its way through,
only to be plucked

before its season.
Too many shoulda-coulda-
wouldas have grown from

broken foundations.
Now all of creation is
groanin' and waitin'

for me to take flight.
Too afraid to fight alone,
I stand here in fear.

Instead of walking
by faith I've allowed my sight
to blind me of God's

true vision of love.
He saw beyond the years of
anguish I would face

the forbidden fruit
I'd taste and the war that keeps
raging in my flesh.

He still knows what's best.
So in those times when I want
to break out and run

I tend to fall back
and hide from the ones I love.
Mama always said

"If you love someone
too much, you just might lose them".
And daddy taught me

with every action
how to use and abuse them.
You think I'm tough now?

I was cold as ice
back then and could care less 'bout
you and your feelings.

It was all about
me and what made me happy,
or at least content.

Looking back at life
I just wanted commitment,
something that would last.

Something to erase
the bitterness of my past.
I wanted to live

the life I dreamed of,
a life worth waking up to.
Guess I expected

perfection from the
moment we said "I do" but
I wasn't perfect.

How could I expect
something from him that I still
needed to become?

I couldn't love him
because I didn't love me.
I didn't love me

'cause I failed to see
beyond *La trials* that I faced.
I shamed my own name

in an attempt to
protect the one thing I had;
my integrity.

When I finally
learned humility, I found
my identity.

I am Agape;
God's unconditional love.
For better or worse,

I can still love you
'cause I refuse to rehearse
the pain of our past.

Now that my future
is in God's hands, I have no
plans to wait on you.

I wrote my vision
and made it plain enough for
my man to follow.

That's means if you're mine,
you'll find your way back. If not,
then get out the way!

With You

Good times are short lived.
So I thank God for every
moment I'm with you.

Without a touch you
melt my heart and soul away,
leaving me naked.

Emotionally,
that is. With words you strip me
right down to my core

and expose feelings
I so often try to hide.
But when you're inside

I can't help but shine
'cause you leave me with a glow
that let's others know

that I just left your
presence. Wrecked by the essence
of your warm embrace,

I don't know if I'm
trippin' or fallin' but I
know I want some more.

You've ravished my heart
and you'll forever be the
Lover of my soul.

How deep is your love?
It extends beyond my flesh.
Beyond the natural.

Beyond what we call
laws of attraction. Beyond
the words and actions

of those who claim to
love me, yet leave me empty
after they've been filled.

Now I'm left longing,
seeking for their attention.
Confused love with lust,

and my hope with trust,
thinking I could be complete
with them in my life.

It was all a lie
but in you I've found the truth.
You are the answer.

You are the cure to
broken hearts and broken dreams.
The pieces of me

no one else has seen.
None could ever reach the depths
of my thirsty soul.

None could fill this hole,
but you hit the spot. Only
You can fill the voids.

One moment with You
makes up for all of the time
I wasted with them.

About the Author

Sonya L. Williams is a freelance writer, publisher, author, and spoken word artist. Her previous published books include *Ice Breakers, 'Til Death Do Us Part* (Volumes I and II), and *Shawty Du Write Haiku*.

As a spoken word artist, Sonya also known as Mz Agape, often expresses her passion for love and romance through poetry. At the 2013 Spoken Word Billboard Awards, she had the honor of being voted Female Expressionist of the Year for her romantic poem titled *Nights Like This*.

For more information about publications and performances, call, write, email or visit the websites listed below:

Sonya L. Williams
PO Box 4654 Woodbridge, VA. 22194
641-715-3900 Ext. 973217

Booking.MzAgape@gmail.com
SonyaLWilliams.Author@gmail.com
http://agapeluv.wix.com/authorsonyalwilliams
http://agapeluv.wix.com/mzagapespokenword
www.Facebook.com/MzSonyaAgape
www.Twitter.com/MzAgape

www.ingramcontent.com/pod-product-compliance
Lightning Source LLC
Chambersburg PA
CBHW060431050426
42449CB00009B/2245